Illustrators
Bruce Hedges
Ken Tunell

Editorial Intern
Gisela Lee

Editorial Project Manager
Ina Massler Levin, M.A.

Editor in Chief
Sharon Coan, M.S. Ed.

Art Director
Elayne Roberts

Art Coordination Assistant
Cheri Macoubrie Wilson

Cover Artist
Larry Bauer

Product Manager
Phil Garcia

Imaging
Alfred Lau
James Edward Grace

Publishers
Rachelle Cracchiolo, M.S. Ed.
Mary Dupuy Smith, M.S. Ed.

20TH C...
BRAIN TEASERS
CHALLENGING

Author
Cynthia Holzschuher

Teacher Created Materials, Inc.
6421 Industry Way
Westminster, CA 92683
www.teachercreated.com

©1998 Teacher Created Materials, Inc.
Reprinted, 2000
Made in U.S.A.
ISBN-1-57690-217-X

Teacher
Created
Materials

TABLE OF CONTENTS

INTRODUCTION

The Brain Teaser series provides ways to exercise and develop brain power! Each page stands alone and can be used as a quick and easy filler activity. The pages can be distributed to students as individual worksheets or made into transparencies for presentation to the entire class at once. The activities are especially useful in helping students develop the following:

- Logic and other critical thinking skills
- Creative thinking skills
- Research skills
- Spelling skills
- General vocabulary and knowledge

This book of *20th Century Brain Teasers* can be used in conjunction with TCM 2100, *The 20th Century,* or answers can be found in any current encyclopedia or reference book like *Chronicle of the 20th Century* (DK, 1995). Some of the puzzles include a word bank for students who may need assistance completing the page. You may block out or fold under the word banks before duplicating to make the puzzles more difficult.

These materials can be used with a United States social studies curriculum to introduce and reinforce knowledge. Current, accurate data has been used in this book as much as possible.

We hope you and your students will have great fun learning more about the people and events of the twentieth century in the United States.

SCRAMBLED NAMES

The names of twelve people from the 1900s have been split into two-letter segments. The letters of the segments are in order, but the segments are scrambled. Put the pieces together to identify the personality. *Clues are given in parenthesis:*

1. ET HS TA IZ AB EL NT ON (women's rights) _____

2. YR OO VE DD LT TE SE (president)_____

3. HI ND GA ND AS HA MO (world leader—India) _____

4. IN EI BE AL RT NS TE (scientist) _____

5. UN SI GM DF RE UD (psychologist) _____

6. DK RU AR DY IP NG LI (author) _____

7. AS BL PA OP IC SO (artist)_____

8. GE LL WI RO RS (performer) _____

9. AN JA RV NA IS (Mother's Day) _____

10. DR AN EW RN CA EG IE (philanthropist) _____

11. WI UR LB WR HT IG (inventor) _____

12. CY MA GO NT ME UD LU MO RY (author) _____

THREE OF A KIND

Below are various categories relating to the 1900s. List three or more people, places, or important dates associated with each category.

1. suffragettes_____

2. Temperance Movement _____

3. Nobel Prize winners _____

4. sports _____

5. artists _____

6. writers _____

7. world leaders _____

8. athletes _____

9. scientists _____

10. inventions _____

11. Industrial Revolution_____

12. political revolutions and wars _____

13. explorers_____

14. presidential assassination _____

15. Hawaii_____

ANALOGIES

To complete an analogy, you must first determine the relationship between the given items. The relationship may be person to birthplace, place to event, inventor to invention, etc. They are read as follows:

Du Bois:NAACP::Robert Baden-Powell:Boy Scouts

(Du Bois is to NAACP as Robert Baden-Powell is to Boy Scouts)

1. Wright Brothers:airplane::Henry Ford:_____

2 Susan B. Anthony:suffrage::Carry Nation:_____

3. William McKinley:Ohio::Theodore Roosevelt:_____

4. Davis Cup:tennis::World Cup:_____

5. dirigible:airship::_____:armored landship

6. Einstein:Germany::Pavlov:_____

7. Planck:quantum theory::_____:theory of relativity

Rudyard Kipling

8. Rudyard Kipling:*The Jungle Book*::Beatrix Potter:_____

9. Picasso:_____::Cassatt:Impressionism

10. Edison:kinetophone::Marconi:_____

11. Anna Jarvis:Mother's Day::Sonora Dodd:_____

12. United States:_____::Australia:Aborigines

13. cricket:England::baseball:_____

14. Boer War:South Africa::Boxer Rebellion:_____

Ivan Pavlov

15. Charlie Gibson:fashion design::Florenz Ziegfeld:_____

AUSTRALIA

Australia became an independent nation on January 1, 1901. Fill in the blanks to complete the words.
When read from top to bottom, the word made by the underlined letters will have something to do with
Australia.

```
                R   O   P   E
         M      U   S   E
EXAMPLE: S   A  T   E   L   T
         A   C  B   S   H   P
         C   A     A   I   E
         A   S  C   S   H   T
         S     K   I       E
                               P
```

1.
```
HO ____ E
D I ____ T
P A ____ N
D I ____ H
B O ____ K
S E ____ D
D E ____ P
T U ____ N
HO ____ T
```
the first white
inhabitants

2.
```
C ____ N D Y
A ____ O U T
F ____ L D S
F ____ R O W
A ____ G N S
A ____ A I N
B ____ K E R
S ____ E A K
M ____ E T S
A ____ K E D
```
native
Australians

3.
```
____ A R E
____ C H E
____ E C K
____ I R D
____ A C H
____ E A D
____ I N G
____ L S O
```
Australia's
capital city

4.
```
B E ____ T
R A ____ E T
S E ____ T S
H A ____ S D
N E ____ D
W E ____ T
```
Australia
has six of these

5.
```
S ____ A R
G I ____ O D
I ____ C H
S ____ O P
D ____ P S
O ____ L Y
T ____ S T
S ____ A P
S ____ A Y
```
Australia
is a country
and a ____.

6.
```
C A ____ I N
B A ____ N S
P A ____ N T
B I ____ E S
G R ____ I N
S H ____ P S
S E ____ D S
```
Australia was
granted
independence
from _____.

7.
```
W I ____ G L E
P O ____ D L E
I S ____ A N D
S A ____ D L E
```
_____ was
discovered in
1851.

8.
```
S T A R ____
R E A D ____
D A T E ____
G R E E ____
G L O B ____
P A R T ____
```
a large
Australian
city

6

R.I.P.

Here are sayings, or epitaphs, that may have appeared on the tombstones of famous artists, writers, and musicians from the 1900s. Read the clues and fill in their names. Use a reference book to add the year each one died.

1. This person is best known for colorful depictions of entertainers in Paris.

    Here lies _____ (1864 – _____)

2. This French Impressionist painter helped develop the style known as "synthetism."

    Here lies _____ (1848 – _____)

3. This American painter is best known for a portrait of his mother.

    Here lies _____ (1834 – _____)

4. This French sculptor designed the Statue of Liberty.

    Here lies _____ (1834 – _____)

5. This French author wrote *Around the World in Eighty Days*.

    Here lies _____ (1828 – _____)

6. This Norwegian poet and playwright is best remembered for his play *A Doll's House*.

    Here lies _____ (1828 – _____)

7. This French Impressionist is best known for his landscape paintings.

    Here lies _____ (1839 – _____)

8. This Russian composer who wrote *Scheherazade* was once a teacher of Igor Stravinsky.

    Here lies _____ (1844 – _____)

9. This person is the American author of Uncle Remus stories.

    Here lies _____ (1848 – _____)

10. This Czech composer's symphonies were inspired by American folk music themes.

    Here lies _____ (1841 – _____)

HEADLINES

Use a reference book to help you find the people or places referred to in each of these stories.

1. _____ Author's work, *The Wonderful Wizard of Oz,* Published (1900)

2. _____ Retiring Steel Baron Gives Away Fortune (1901)

3. _____ Indian Territory Given to Settlers (1901)

4. _____ President Shot: Assassin Arrested (1901)

5. _____ U.S. Pays $40 Million for Right to Dig in Central America (1902)

6. _____ President Helps Settle Coal Strike (1902)

7. _____ Stock Exchange Opens with Ticker Tape Parade (1903)

8. _____ Engineer Will Manufacture Horseless Carriage (1903)

9. _____ First World Series Won by American League Team (1903)

10. _____ President Inaugurated During Snowstorm (1909)

11. _____ Explorer Plants U.S. Flag on North Pole (1909)

12. _____ Apache Leader Dies at 80 (1909)

13. _____ Olympics Open in British Capital (1908)

14. _____ Nobel Prize Goes to Writer in India (1907)

15. _____ European Immigrants Continue to Enter U.S. (1907)

Word Bank

• Ellis Island	• Panama	• Theodore Roosevelt
• London	• Oklahoma Territory	• Henry Ford
• Robert Peary	• Lyman Frank Baum	• William Howard Taft
• Boston	• Andrew Carnegie	• Geronimo
• New York City	• William McKinley	• Rudyard Kipling

A TALE OF TWO PRESIDENTS 1910-1919

From 1910 to 1919, two men had the honor and responsibility of leading the United States of America as president. They also shared the following letters in their names: D R W O L I. A list of their statements, activities, and accomplishments follows. Your challenge is to identify the presidents and write their names next to their activities, statements, and accomplishments.

Activities and Accomplishments	President
1. President of Princeton University	_____
2. Governor of the Philippines	_____
3. Governor of New Jersey	_____
4. Chief Justice of the U.S. Supreme Court	_____
5. Established the U.S. Postal System	_____
6. Vigorously prosecuted the Sherman Antitrust Law	_____
7. Served as U.S. Secretary of War	_____
8. Established the Federal Reserve Banking System	_____
9. Founded the League of Nations	_____
10. Promoted "Dollar Diplomacy"	_____
11. Elected president because "He kept us out of war"	_____
12. Opposed "Dollar Diplomacy"	_____
13. Asked Congress to declare war against Germany	_____
14. Established Federal Children's Bureau	_____
15. Established Parcel Post	_____
16. Awarded Nobel Prize for peace	_____
17. Said "The world must be made safe for democracy"	_____
18. Established full territorial government for Alaska	_____
19. Established U.S. Department of Labor	_____
20. Only man ever to lead two of the three branches of U.S. government	_____

THE GREAT WAR

Fill in the blanks to complete the words. When read from top to bottom, the word made by the underlined letters will have something to do with World War I. The first one has been done for you.

1
```
S  H  A̲  P  E
H  O  L̲  L  E  Y
D  E  L̲  A  Y  S
R  E  I̲  L  D  S
S  A  E̲  A  D  E
W  A  S̲  T  E
```

2
```
S  ___  O  P
L  ___  N  D  Y
O  ___  L  I  E  P
S  ___  I  E  D
U  ___  E  P  D
```

3
```
S  L  ___  E  P
C  O  ___  E  S
S  T  ___  A  B  M
S  O  ___  B  S
F  L  ___  E  R
```

4
```
U  ___  H  E  R
Q  ___  E  E  N  R
A  ___  O  U  T  T
A  ___  B  E  N  R
P  ___  I  N  S  W
A  ___  R  O  W  D
W  ___  P  E  I  D
U  ___  T  I  T  L
M  ___  L  T  S
```

5
```
S  T  ___  N  D
F  A  ___  M  S  S
T  O  ___  B  S  S
M  A  ___  B  E
```

6
```
___  O  R  C  E
___  R  D  E  R  E
___  A  N  G  E  Y
___  A  R  R  Y  Y
___  V  E  R  Y
```

7
```
R  E  ___  O  V  E
C  H  ___  R  R  M  O  N  S
M  I  ___  R  I  O  N  E  R  G
F  A  ___  I  N  L  D
B  E  ___  O  L  D
```

8
```
T  H  A  ___
T  A  R  E  ___  S
A  S  T  A  ___  A
B  H  R  U  G  ___
B  H  U  I  O  ___
R  I  O  ___
```

9
```
D  ___  R  T  Y
U  ___  D  E  R  Y  E
E  ___  E  S  T  R  R
T  ___  S  T  E  S
O  ___  O  V  E  N
S  ___  V  E
```

10
```
M  ___  R  R  Y
S  ___  A  R  E  Y
O  ___  H  R  E  S  R
P  ___  N  T  P  S  E
S  ___  O  P  S
S  ___  I  P
```

11
```
___  R  I  L  L
___  V  E  R  Y  L
___  I  D  G  E  R  Y
___  O  V  E  R  Y
___  N  G  R  E  Y
___  E  V  E  R  R
___  O  U  R  S
```

12
```
B  U  L  ___
G  A  L  L  ___
D  O  L  L  A
W  A  L  L  M
M  A  M  ___
K  I  L  S  ___
M  I  S
```

LABOR REFORM

Use the diagrams to decode these changes in early labor practices.

A	B	C
D	E	F
G	H	I

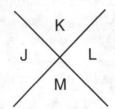

N•	O•	P•
Q•	R•	S•
T•	U•	V•

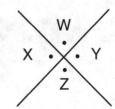

Example: PICKET LINE

1.

2.

3.

4.

5.

6.

7.

8.

9.

10.

TELEGRAMS

Years before we had fax machines and e-mail, people sent urgent messages around the world over telegraph lines. Telegrams were sent in Morse code, received at a central office, printed on paper, and delivered by messengers. Fill in the words that complete the following telegrams. The word "stop" was used as a period because Morse code did not include punctuation.

1.	1910	"Edison invention revolutionizes entertainment industry stop Moviegoers enjoy _____"
2.	1914	"First ship passes from Pacific to Atlantic stop Americans cheer opening of _____"
3.	1915	"Passenger liner torpedoed killing 1,200 stop German sub sinks _____"
4.	1917	"Tsar Nicholas II abdicates throne stop Revolutionaries install _____ as new leader"
5.	1912	"Luxury liner hits iceberg stop 1,517 people lost in sinking of _____"
6.	1912	"Native American athlete wins medals in pentathlon and decathlon at 1912 _____"
7.	1910	"Spokane woman's efforts successful stop June 10 will be first _____"
8.	1918	"Influenza _____ kills 20 million people worldwide stop Hospitals cannot handle numbers"
9.	1919	"Women's Christian Temperance Union campaigns against purchase and consumption of _____ stop Legislation pending"
10.	1917	"Women suffragettes take stand for_____"
11.	1919	"Paris Peace Conference opposes Wilson's Fourteen Points stop _____ seems unlikely"
12.	1916	"Legislature passes Keating-Owen Act stop Federal ban on _____"

12

WHO DONE IT?

Solve these mysteries with names of famous people from the 1910s. Study the clues and then use a reference book to help find the answers.

1. The Mona Lisa (da Vinci masterpiece) was stolen from the Louvre in Paris. (1911)
   Who done it? _____

2. This Norwegian explorer was the first to reach the South Pole. (1911)
   Who done it? _____

3. This female scientist won her second Nobel Prize in 1911.
   Who done it? _____

4. This doctor eliminated yellow fever and malaria at the site of the building of the Panama Canal. (1913)
   Who done it? _____

5. Archduke Ferdinand and his wife were gunned down in the streets of Sarajevo. (1914)
   Who done it? _____

6. Former heavyweight fighter James J. Jeffries came out of retirement but was defeated by this boxer. (1910)
   Who done it? _____

7. The British liner *Lusitania* was sunk in 1915.
   Who done it? _____

8. Tsar Nicholas and his family were executed in 1918.
   Who done it? _____

9. Mata Hari was executed for espionage in 1917.
   Who done it? _____

10. This German physicist won the Nobel Prize for the quantum theory in 1918.
    Who done it? _____

11. This leader introduced postwar Italy to a new political organization.
    Who done it? _____

12. A peace treaty ending World War I was signed at Versailles, France, in 1919.
    Who done it? _____

13. An overworked U.S. president abandons a national tour due to poor health in 1919.
    Who done it? _____

14. The Greek king abdicated the throne to avoid a provisional war government.
    Who done it? _____

15. Thousands of Armenians were murdered in Turkey. (1915)
    Who done it? _____

DISASTER ON THE HIGH SEAS

Analyze these groups of letters to solve the puzzles. They are in order, no letters have been omitted, but they cannot be read left to right. Patterns may be horizontal or vertical. Pay close attention to the clues provided.

1

```
J   B   L   E   T   U   S
D   N   A   T   I   M   N
L   I   C   X   Y   O   H
```

It was thought that this luxury liner could not sink.

2

```
Y   C   T   H   B   P   D
E   A   A   I   U   E   O
J   R   P   A   K   N   Z
```

This ship responded to the luxury liner's SOS.

3

```
E   I   L   A   C   F   N
Q   F   O   R   N   J   E
U   S   X   A   I   A   K
```

This ship did not receive the luxury liner's signal for help.

4

```
Y   O   Y   W   E   N   L
Z   R   K   C   I   T   Y
C   J   M   A   X   P   Q
```

The original destination of the luxury liner was for this American city.

5

```
X   B   E   E   G   A   E
L   E   C   R   N   I   K
M   R   I   O   A   G   M
O   G   S   U   D   Z   N
```

Hitting this caused the disaster.

6

```
R   C   I   A   I   W   G
P   A   N   R   T   A   H
Q   P   E   D   H   L   D
J   T   D   S   X   I   B
Z   A   W   M   Y   K   O
```

This captain went down with his ship.

7

```
D   K   P   S   A   P   H
R   L   D   T   F   J   L
S   M   N   I   L   N   M
Z   W   A   R   E   O   C
T   A   L   E   B   U   D
```

The luxury liner was built in this city and country.

8

```
M   T   S   N   H   J   G
N   O   A   J   O   E   I
Y   R   B   A   J   U   Z
K   F   O   C   P   W   H
```

This American millionaire was a passenger who died on the ship.

PICTURE PUZZLE

Complete this challenging puzzle by cutting out the individual pieces to form a picture of an important symbol of the 1910s. Glue the completed puzzle onto colored construction paper. Who is the mystery person, and when did he first become a part of American history?

SOUND AND SILENCE

Motion pictures (or the "movies") achieved great popularity in the 1920s. It was this decade that saw the advent of sound in motion pictures, first called "talkies." In 1926, Warner Brothers Studio introduced the first really practical sound films using the process called Vitaphone. Some of the great figures of early silent films successfully made the shift to sound but some did not. The following is a list of memorable figures who achieved fame in those transitional years along with some famous film titles associated with them over the years. See if you can match the person with the film and identify the movie as silent or sound.

Person	Film	Sound or Silent
_____1. Al Jolson	A. *Our Hearts Were Young and Gay*	_____
_____2. Walt Disney	B. *Nanook of the North*	_____
_____3. Charlie Chaplin	C. *Steamboat Willie*	_____
_____4. Dorothy Gish	D. *The Iron Horse*	_____
_____5. Douglas Fairbanks	E. *The Sheik*	_____
_____6. Lillian Gish	F. *The Gold Rush*	_____
_____7. Buster Keaton	G. *The Freshman*	_____
_____8. Harold Lloyd	H. *The Mark of Zorro*	_____
_____9. Mary Pickford	I. *The Jazz Singer*	_____
_____10. Rudolph Valentino	J. *The Birth of a Nation*	_____
_____11. John Ford	K. *Sherlock, Jr.*	_____
_____12. Robert Flaherty	L. *Coquette*	_____

CREATE-A-WORD
SOCIAL ISSUES

Choose a part of a word from each column to form a new word about social issues in the twenties.
Each part may be used only once. The first part of each word is in Column A. Write the new words in
the blanks.

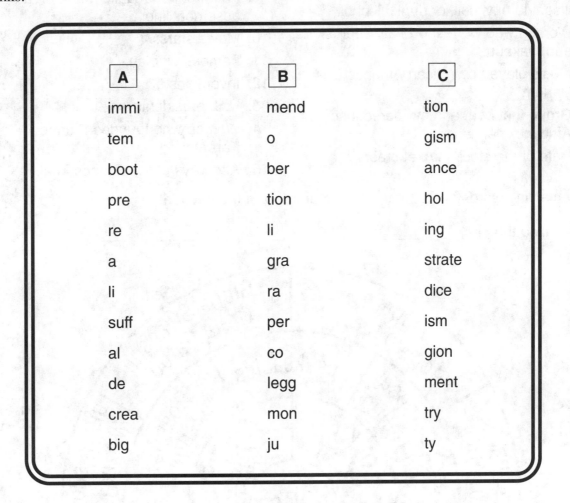

A	B	C
immi	mend	tion
tem	o	gism
boot	ber	ance
pre	tion	hol
re	li	ing
a	gra	strate
li	ra	dice
suff	per	ism
al	co	gion
de	legg	ment
crea	mon	try
big	ju	ty

1. _____

2. _____

3. _____

4. _____

5. _____

6. _____

7. _____

8. _____

9. _____

10. _____

11. _____

12. _____

THE TWENTIES

Cross out the words associated with this era.

1. A gangster who made millions of dollars selling illegal alcohol.
2. The 18th Amendment which made it illegal to buy, sell, or drink alcohol.
3. Women who wore short hair, short skirts, and makeup.
4. Music played by African Americans in Harlem.
5. Group that beat and murdered innocent African Americans.
6. Date of the stock market crash.
7. Clubs that served illegal alcohol.
8. Sports heroes.
9. The first automobile made on an assembly line.
10. Movie stars.
11. Famous women.
12. Inventions.
13. U.S. presidents.
14. Women who founded Planned Parenthood.
15. Attorneys at the Scopes Trial.

The remaining words are a common nickname given the decade.

It was called the _____ _____

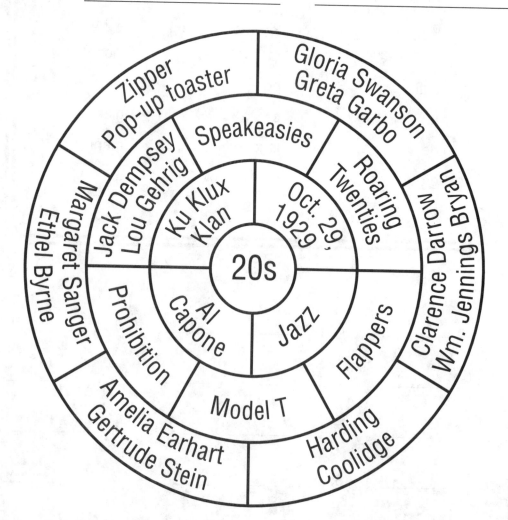

PRODUCT SLOGANS

Many of the products introduced in the 1920s are still popular today. Match these slogans to the products they might have advertised. Use the pictures as clues for some of the products.

1. It's faster than buttons, and it won't fall off!

   _____

2. For a clean, fresh taste, try this chewing sensation.

   _____

3. This will protect your small cuts from dirt and germs.

   _____

4. These new, disposable handkerchiefs are convenient and inexpensive.

   _____

5. This product will stick to paper instantly, no more waiting for messy glue.

   _____

6. Try America's newest way to eat spuds!

   _____

7. Fresher than canned foods—they go right from the freezer into your recipes.

   _____

8. Imagine yourself in a new, curly "do."

   _____

9. Try this new chocolate-covered ice cream on a stick.

   _____

10. This tasty fruit spread is perfect on your morning toast.

   _____

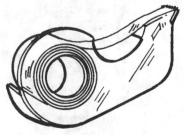

THREE CLUES

Write the name of a famous person for each set of clues. *There are more names listed in the word bank than are needed.*

1. Red Sox, home run hitter, Yankees _____

2. 1919 World Series, indictment, gambling _____

3. 29th president, Republican, normalcy _____

4. murderers, Italians, guilty _____

5. Egypt, tomb, archaeology _____

6. Russian Revolution, Bolshevik, Gorky _____

7. Tennessee, evolution, biology teacher _____

8. magician, escape artist, water torture _____

9. New York, Paris, solo flight _____

10. Cotton Club, Big Band, piano music _____

11. flight, Atlantic Ocean, first woman _____

12. emperor, Japan, world peace _____

13. French, fashion designer, simplicity _____

14. explorer, Antarctica, polar flight _____

15. bacteriologist, penicillin, bread mold _____

Word Bank

- Babe Ruth
- Alexander Fleming
- "Shoeless" Joe Jackson
- Commander Richard Byrd
- Warren G. Harding
- Coco Chanel
- Sacco and Vanzetti
- Emperor Hirohito
- Tutankhamen
- Amelia Earhart
- Vladimir Lenin
- Duke Ellington
- Charles Lindbergh
- John Scopes
- Harry Houdini
- Benito Mussolini
- William Jennings Bryan
- Satchel Paige
- Langston Hughes
- Charlie Chaplin

Satchel Paige

Charles Lindbergh

Babe Ruth

EGYPTIAN EXCAVATION

Use the diagrams to decode these facts about King Tut's Tomb.

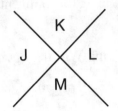

A	B	C
D	E	F
G	H	I

(K J · L M cross diagram)

N•	O•	P•
Q•	R•	S•
T•	U•	V•

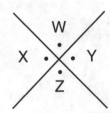

(W X · · Y Z cross diagram)

Example: ⊡⌐⌙⊡⌞⛝⌞⌐⌐⌙⊓⌐ SARCOPHAGUS

1. _____

2. _____

3. _____

4. _____

5. _____

6. _____

7. _____

8. _____

9. _____

10. _____

11. _____

ANALOGIES

To complete an analogy, you must first determine the relationship between the given items. The relationship may be person to birthplace, place to event, inventor to invention, etc. They are read as follows:

Igor Sikorsky:helicopter::Sir Frank Whittle:jet engine

(Igor Sikorsky is to helicopter as Sir Frank Whittle is to jet engine)

1. Herbert Hoover:Stanford::Franklin Roosevelt:_____

2. Civilian Conservation Corps:parks::Public Works Administration:_____

3. Al Capone:_____::John Dillinger:bank robber

4. dust bowl:farmers::stock market crash:_____

5. Pearl Buck:*The Good Earth*::_____:*Gone with the Wind*

6. Joe Louis:boxing::Jesse Owens:_____

7. _____:Benny Goodman::trombone:Glenn Miller

8. *American Gothic*:painting::*This Land Is Your Land*:_____

9. _____:five offspring::twins:two offspring

10. Adolf Hitler:_____::Chiang Kai-shek:China

11. Clark Gable:actor::Greta Garbo:_____

12. mobiles:_____::painting:Thomas Hart Benton

13. Urban League:Mary McLeod Bethune::_____:Marian Anderson

14. Great Depression:Herbert Hoover::New Deal:_____

15. Romeo:Juliet::Edward VIII:_____

TRIVIA

Find the names of famous personalities from the 1930s.

1. This first couple sometimes spoke Chinese to assure having private conversations.

   _____

2. Which presidential couple had four children in their first five years of marriage?

   _____

3. Who was the first woman in the U.S. to earn a college degree in geology?

   _____

4. Which scientist developed products from peanuts, sweet potatoes, and pecans?

   _____

5. Who was the first woman to win the Nobel Peace Prize?

   _____

6. This child star entered politics as an adult.

   _____

7. This singer/songwriter created a style called "talking blues."

   _____

8. Which track and field athlete was the first to go over the high bar headfirst?

   _____

9. This composer of *Peter and the Wolf* died on the same day as Josef Stalin.

   _____

10. Which writer, who won both the Pulitzer and Nobel Prizes, once worked as a maintenance man?

    _____

11. Who was the only king of England ever to abdicate the throne?

    _____

12. This mild-mannered superhero was first introduced in 1930s comic books.

    _____

QUOTES IN CODES

Decode these presidential quotes.

Code	A	B	C	D	E	F	G	H	I	J	K	L	M	N	O	P	Q	R	S	T	U	V	W	X	Y	Z
Key	Y	Z	A	B	C	D	E	F	G	H	I	J	K	L	M	N	O	P	Q	R	S	T	U	V	W	X

" C ejkemgp kp gxgta rqv: C ect kp gxgta ictcig."

—*Herbert Hoover*

"

_____ :

_____ ."

Code	A	B	C	D	E	F	G	H	I	J	K	L	M	N	O	P	Q	R	S	T	U	V	W	X	Y	Z
Key	Z	A	B	C	D	E	F	G	H	I	J	K	L	M	N	O	P	Q	R	S	T	U	V	W	X	Y

" Xf ibwf opuijoh up gfbs cvu gfbs jutfmg."

—*Franklin Roosevelt*

"

_____

_____ ."

Code	A	B	C	D	E	F	G	H	I	J	K	L	M	N	O	P	Q	R	S	T	U	V	W	X	Y	Z
Key	B	C	D	E	F	G	H	I	J	K	L	M	N	O	P	Q	R	S	T	U	V	W	X	Y	Z	A

"Ntq fqdzsdrs oqhlzqx szrj hr sn ots odnokd sn vnqj."

—*Franklin Roosevelt*

"

_____

_____ ."

OLYMPIC COMPETITIONS

Fill in the missing letters to reveal information and highlights of the Olympics in 1932 and 1936.

_____ R O A D   J U M P   J E S S E _____ W E N S

H A M M _____ R   T H R O W   B L A C K   A T H _____ E T E S

M A _____ A T H O N   V I C T O R _____

L U T Z _____ O N G   G O L D _____ E D A L S

H _____ T L E R   H I G H   J U M _____

_____ A Z I S   A M E R _____ C A N S

D E _____ A T H L O N

T R A C K _____ T A R

What words are spelled by the letters in the blanks?

_____   _____

P E N T A T H _____ O N   L O N G   J U _____ P

S H _____ T P U T   F _____ N C I N G

D I _____ C U S   _____ I V I N G

T R _____ C K   D E C _____ T H L O N

B O X I _____ G   W R E S T _____ I N G

R O W I N _____   B A C K _____ T R O K E

R _____ L A Y   R A C E S

W A T E R   P O _____ O

H U R D L _____ S

_____ W I M M I N G

What words are spelled by the letters in the blanks?

_____   _____

WORDS WITHIN WORDS

Use the clues to help you fill in the blanks with a small word. The answers relate to the politics and economics of the 1930s. *Clues are given in parentheses.*

1. G R E __ __   D E __ __ __ __ __ I O N (*economy*)

2. L A B __ __   U N I __ __ S (*economy*)

3. P R O H I __ __ __ I O N (*21st Amendment*)

4. M I G __ __ __ I O N (*Dust Bowl*)

5. __ __ L I __ __ __ T E R (*new aircraft*)

6. H O O V E R V __ __ __ E S (*shanty towns*)

7. U N __ __ __ __ __ __ M E N T (*economy*)

8. P __ __ __ __ __ __ N T (*U.S. leader*)

9. __ __ C I A L   S E C U R __ __ Y (*New Deal*)

10. A __ __ L F   __ __ __ L E R (*German leader*)

CREATIONS OF THE THIRTIES

Use the telephone diagram to help crack the code. Find each number on the telephone and use the dot to indicate the position of the letter which appears above it. See example. A= •2, B= 2̇, C= 2 • (for the two letters not on the telephone, Z=0 and Q=1)

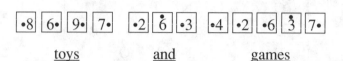

| •8 | 6• | 9• | 7• | | •2 | 6̇ | •3 | | •4 | •2 | •6 | 3̇ | 7• |

toys   and   games

1. | •6 | 6• | 6̇ | 6• | •7 | 6• | 5• | 9• | _____

2. | 9• | 6• | 9• | 6• | _____

3. | 7̇ | 6• | 5• | 5• | 3̇ | 7 | | 7• | 5̇ | •2 | •8 | 3̇ | 7• |

   _____   _____

4. | •5 | 8̇ | •6 | •7 | | 7̇ | 6• | •7 | 3 | _____

5. | 3• | 7̇ | 6• | 0 | 3̇ | 6̇ | | 3• | 6• | 6• | •3 |

   _____   _____

6. | 7• | •7 | •2 | •6 | _____

7. | •9 | 6• | 6̇ | •3 | 3̇ | 7 | | 2̇ | 7 | 3̇ | •2 | •3 |

   _____

8. | 7• | 6̇ | 6• | •9 | | •9 | 4̇ | 4• | •8 | 3̇ | | •2 | 6̇ | •3 | | •8 | 4̇ | 3̇ |

   | 7• | 3̇ | 8• | 3̇ | 6̇ | | •3 | •9 | •2 | 7̇ | 3• | 7• |

   _____   _____   _____

   _____   _____

9. | •8 | 3̇ | 5• | 3̇ | 8• | 4• | 7• | 4• | 6• | 6̇ | _____

10. | 7• | 8̇ | •7 | 3̇ | 7̇ | •6 | •2 | 6̇ | _____

27

WORLD WAR II

Analyze these groups of letters to solve the puzzles. They are in order, no letters have been omitted, but they cannot be read left to right. Patterns may be horizontal or vertical. Pay close attention to the clues provided.

1
C	X	Y	Z	B	J	G
P	A	R	B	O	H	E
M	E	L	R	R	I	A
O	P	H	A	X	D	K

Bombed by Japan

_____

2
N	P	U	O	I	Z	Y
C	O	O	N	T	N	I
L	N	C	I	A	U	R
F	S	G	N	R	O	S

Supply and demand

_____

3
X	S	O	R	I	B	A
Y	I	E	T	U	N	U
L	R	E	H	E	Q	K
J	I	V	E	A	T	G
S	R	E	T	U	V	W

Symbolized working women

_____

4
Q	W	I	N	S	J	N
R	C	N	O	T	A	I
S	H	U	R	C	U	L
F	L	L	I	H	Z	X

British leader

_____

5
Q	F	N	R	L	T	E
Z	R	I	O	E	A	O
J	A	L	O	V	G	U
M	N	K	S	E	N	D

American leader

_____

6
B	X	A	M	T	J	Y
D	I	S	P	O	X	W
C	S	R	E	W	A	E
A	T	U	Q	Y	Z	X

Germany, Japan, and Italy formed this alliance

_____

7
Z	U	O	D	J	A	Y
H	G	L	A	S	M	L
I	T	R	A	C	A	K
B	H	U	R	K	T	G

Famous American general who vowed "I shall return"

_____

8
B	S	C	I	L	G	M
Y	T	E	J	N	Q	S
L	A	L	O	P	K	R
T	R	A	N	D	B	D

World War II began when Germany invaded this country.

_____

28

THREE OF A KIND

Below are various categories relating to the 1940s. List three or more people, places, or important dates associated with each category.

1. U.S. war heroes _____

2. war rationed foods _____

3. Nazi concentration camps _____

4. women in the military _____

5. women's fashions _____

6. men's fashions _____

7. jazz musicians _____

8. Big Band vocalists _____

9. artists _____

10. writers _____

11. world leaders _____

12. athletes _____

13. scientists _____

14. cartoons/animation _____

15. inventions _____

WORLD WAR II LISTS

The events, items, and people listed here were all significant to the war effort around the world. Read each list and fill in the titles.

1. _____
   United States
   England
   Russia
   Churchill
   Eisenhower

2. _____
   Germany
   Italy
   Japan
   Tojo
   Eichmann

3. _____
   fat man
   little boy
   Nagasaki
   Hiroshima
   nuclear fallout

4. _____
   Rosie the Riveter
   rationing
   victory garden
   war bonds
   selective service

5. _____
   meat
   sugar
   butter
   coffee
   gasoline

6. _____
   Dwight Eisenhower
   Douglas MacArthur
   George Patton
   Omar Bradley
   Ernie Pyle

7. _____
   Hideki Tojo
   Joseph Stalin
   Benito Mussolini
   Adolf Hitler
   Winston Churchill

8. _____
   spitfire
   B-17
   Stuka
   B-29
   Messerschmitt

9. _____
   Dunkirk
   D-Day
   Pearl Harbor
   Battle of the Bulge
   Kursk

10. _____
   German camps
   "Jewish problem"
   prisoners
   ovens
   six million killed

READ ALL ABOUT IT

Use a reference book to help you fill in the date for each of these events.

1. _____ **FDR Declares War on Japan**
Pearl Harbor Bombed

2. _____ **FDR Inaugurated to 4th Term**

3. _____ **Men 21–36 Must Register for Draft**

4. _____ **U.S. Troops Land at Iwo Jima**

5. _____ **FDR Dies—Truman Takes Oath**

6. _____ **Winston Churchill Becomes**
Britain's Prime Minister

7. _____ **Allies Invade Western Europe on D-Day**

8. _____ **Soviet Forces Free Jews at Auschwitz**

9. _____ **Hitler Commits Suicide in Berlin**

10. _____ **U.S. Drops A-Bomb—Japan Surrenders**

THAT'S ENTERTAINMENT!

Fill in the missing letters to reveal information about entertainment in the 1940s

JITTER _____ UG

GLENN M _____ LLER

SWIN _____

_____ E-BOP

J _____ ZZ

FRANK SI _____ ATRA

AN _____ REW SISTERS

_____ USICALS

D _____ KE ELLINGTON

BOBBY _____ OXERS

D _____ ZZY GILLESPIE

BING _____ ROSBY

What words are spelled by the letters in the blanks?

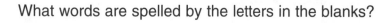

_____   _____   _____

COS _____ UMES

C _____ OREOGRAPHY

CITIZ _____ N KANE

BRO _____ DWAY

DIREC _____ OR

G _____ NE KELLY

O _____ SON WELLES

What word is spelled by the letters in the blanks? _____

32

MADE IN THE U.S.A.

The following products were being made in the U.S.A. during the 1940s. Find the products in the puzzle box below. The trick to solving the puzzle is that the words can be found in any direction. None of them are in a straight line. One has been done for you as an example.

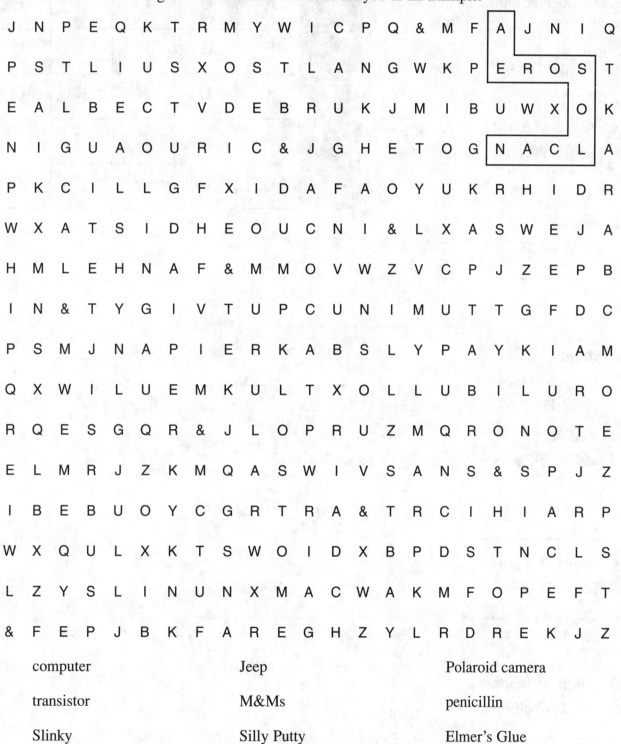

computer	Jeep	Polaroid camera
transistor	M&Ms	penicillin
Slinky	Silly Putty	Elmer's Glue
electric blanket	aerosol can	Morton Salt

HAPPENED IN THE '50S

Use the diagram to decipher the code. The first number is from the vertical line on the left. The second is from the horizontal line across the top.

Example: w = 53
　　　　　 d = 14

Example: 13-35-32-14　　　53-11-43
　　　　　　　cold　　　　　　　　war

	1	2	3	4	5
1	A	B	C	D	E
2	F	G	H	I	J
3	K	L	M	N	O
4	P	Q	R	S	T
5	U	V	W	X	YZ

1. people

12-11-12-55　　　　12-35-35-33-15-43-44

_____　　_____

12-15-11-45　　　　22-15-34-15-43-11-45-24-35-34

_____　　_____

2. states

23-11-53-11-24-24　　_____

11-32-11-44-31-11　　_____

3. medicine

41-35-32-24-35　　　52-11-13-13-24-34-15

_____　　_____

31-24-14-34-15-55　45-43-11-34-44-41-32-11-34-45

_____　　_____

4. entertainment

13-35-32-35-43　　　45-15-32-15-52-24-44-24-35-34

_____　　_____

33-11-25-35-43　　　32-15-11-22-51-15　　　12-11-44-15-12-11-32-32

_____　　_____　　　_____

5. religious leaders

12-24-32-32-55　　　22-43-11-23-11-33

_____　　_____

41-35-41-15　　　　25-35-23-34　　　41-11-51-32　　　54-54-24-24-24

_____　　_____　　_____　　_____

KIDS' STUFF

Kids' Stuff puzzles may include names of games, toys, entertainment, or food products from the period. The first number is from the vertical line on the left. The second is from the horizontal line across the top. Use the diagram to decipher the code.

Example: w = 53
         d = 14

Example: 45-15-32-15-52-24-44-24-35-34
                    <u>television</u>

	1	2	3	4	5
1	A	B	C	D	E
2	F	G	H	I	J
3	K	L	M	N	O
4	P	Q	R	S	T
5	U	V	W	X	YZ

(1) 21-43-24-44-12-15-15 _____

(2) 33-11-14   33-11-22-11-55-24-34-15 _____ _____

(3) 12-11-43-12-24-15   14-35-32-32

_____   _____

(4) 43-35-13-31 '34' 43-35-32-32 _____

(5) 45-52   14-24-34-34-15-43 _____ _____

(6) 23-51-32-11   23-35-35-41 _____ _____

(7) 44-13-43-11-12-12-32-15 _____

(8) 13-23-11-43-32-35-45-45-15-'44   53-15-12

_____   _____

(9) 14-43.   44-15-51-44-44 _____ _____

(10) 25-24-21   41-15-11-34-51-45   12-51-45-45-15-43

_____   _____   _____

ALASKA AND HAWAII

Alaska and Hawaii became states in 1959. Read each clue. Write A if the statement is about Alaska, H if it is about Hawaii.

1. _____ Queen Liliuokalani

2. _____ Mauna Loa

3. _____ Juneau

4. _____ Eskimos

5. _____ William Seward

6. _____ Nene (state bird)

7. _____ Captain James Cook

8. _____ glaciers

9. _____ pineapples

10. _____ volcanoes

11. _____ January 3, 1959

12. _____ eight small islands

13. _____ willow ptarmigan (state bird)

14. _____ hibiscus (state flower)

15. _____ forget-me-not (state flower)

16. _____ August 21, 1959

17. _____ Mount McKinley

18. _____ North to the Future (state motto)

19. _____ Aleutian Islands

20. _____ Polynesian cultures

Alaska

Hawaii

POPULAR MUSIC
REBUS WRITING

Decode the pictures to reveal the names of songs or musicians of the fifties.

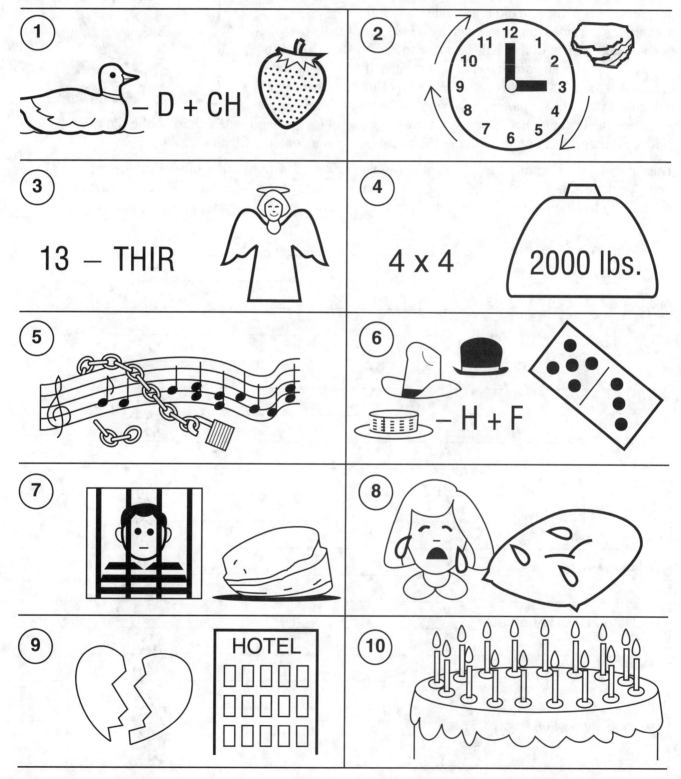

A HERO FROM THE FIFTIES

During the mid-1950s the United States witnessed the development of an extraordinary leader—a man who called out to the conscience of all America. He was a Christian minister whose congregation was not restricted to the rooms within a church. He called out to all peoples of this diverse, multiethnic nation—religious or nonreligious, inside churches or outside. Indeed, his call was to all humankind. Martin Luther King, Jr. rose to become a great symbol of justice and human equality, earning for himself an ever-lasting memory in the annals of this nation. Many politicians have been quick to take credit for passing civil rights laws, but Martin Luther King was the inspirational leader who took this country by the hand to lead it to do the right thing—to "judge all humans not by the color of their skin but by the content of their character."

The following is a list of dates, places, and people associated with Martin Luther King's eventful life (which extended beyond the 1950s, of course) in the service of the great cause of human equality. See if you can identify them with a few words describing how they were connected to the great hero.

1. Mohandas Gandhi _____

_____

2. Coretta Scott _____

_____

3. Rosa Parks_____

_____

4. SCLC _____

_____

5. Birmingham, Alabama _____

_____

6. James Earl Ray _____

_____

7. Andrew Young _____

_____

8. Ralph David Abernathy _____

_____

9. Selma, Alabama_____

_____

10. Oslo, Norway (1964) _____

_____

IN THE NEWS

Use a reference book to help you find the items referred to in each of these stories.

1. _____ Charlotte Evangelist Returns to Hometown (1958)

2. _____ Quiz Show Caught in Scandal (1958)

3. _____ First Lady Steps Down Gracefully (1953)

4. _____ WWII Hero Named to Head Korean Forces (1950)

5. _____ Island Kingdom Becomes 50th State (1959)

6. _____ Couple Charged with Giving Secrets to Soviets (1951)

7. _____ Woman Arrested for Refusing to Give Up Bus Seat (1955)

8. _____ Amendment Limits Presidential Term (1951)

9. _____ Armistice Signed: Fighting Ends (1953)

10. _____ Arkansas' Central High School Is Integrated (1957)

11. _____ First African American Woman Plays in the U.S. Open (1950)

12. _____ The "Yankee Clipper" Retires from Baseball with 361 Home Runs (1952)

13. _____ U.S. Launches Space Program with Satellite (1958)

14. _____ Anthropologist Discovers Human Fossils in Africa (1959)

15. _____ Plane Crash Kills Three Musicians (1959)

_____

_____

Word Bank

- Buddy Holly
- Ritchie Valens
- J.P. Richardson
- Hawaii
- *Explorer I*
- Mary Leakey
- Little Rock Nine
- Joe DiMaggio
- Korean War
- General Douglas MacArthur
- Bess Truman
- Althea Gibson
- 22nd Amendment
- Billy Graham
- *Twenty-One*
- Rosa Parks
- Ethel and Julius Rosenberg

ANALOGIES

To complete an analogy, you must first determine the relationship between the given items. The relationship may be person to birthplace, place to event, inventor to invention, etc. They are read as follows:

Fats Domino:"Blueberry Hill"::Chuck Berry:"Maybelline"

(Fats Domino is to "Blueberry Hill" as Chuck Berry is to "Maybelline")

1. John Kennedy:Jackie::Lyndon Johnson:_____

2. Golda Meir:_____::John Kennedy:president

3. Marilyn Monroe:actress::Wilma Rudolph:_____

4. Cesar Chavez:California::Martin Luther King, Jr.:_____

5. Roberto Clemente:athlete::Neil Armstrong:_____

6. Charles Schultz:cartoons::Maurice Sendak:_____

7. Indira Ghandi:India::Golda Meir:_____

8. *Peanuts*:_____::100 cans of Campbell's soup:Andy Warhol

9. Neil Armstrong:USA::Valentina Tereshkova:_____

10. Sidney Poitier:_____::Roberto Clemente:Pittsburgh

11. *Where the Wild Things Are*:Maurice Sendak::_____:Nikki Giovanni::*Silent Spring*:_____

12. Dr. Christian Barnard:_____::Louis Washansky:
_____::_____:donor

13. Mao Tse-tung:China::Nikita Khrushchev:_____

14. _____:Soviet Union::Alan Shepard:USA

POPULAR MUSIC

Decode the pictures to reveal the names of songs, groups, or musicians of the sixties.

CATEGORIES

Read the clues and fill in the category.

1. Danang, Haiphong Harbor, Tet Offensive _____

2. Freedom Rides, Sit-Ins, Watts Riots _____

3. Martin Luther King, Jr., John F. Kennedy, Medgar Evers _____

4. Neil Armstrong, Buzz Aldrin, Michael Collins _____

5. magnetron, fan, turntable _____

6. Linus, Snoopy, Lucy _____

7. *Help!, Revolver, A Hard Day's Night* _____

8. Fidel Castro, blockade, Kruschev _____

9. Michael Jordan, Brooke Shields, Whitney Houston _____

10. Sea of Tranquility, Sea of Rains, Sea of Cold _____

11. Harry Belafonte, Ossie Davis, Sidney Poitier _____

12. neon signs, Coca-Cola bottles, Campbell's soup cans _____

13. Medicare, Voting Rights Act, Civil Rights Act _____

14. communes, hippies, Woodstock _____

15. *Catch-22, To Kill a Mockingbird, Slaughterhouse Five* _____

Word Bank

- Vietnam War
- assassinated leaders
- parts of a microwave
- Beatles albums
- celebrities born in the 1960s
- African American actors
- popular literary works
- subjects of Andy Warhol's paintings
- moon landmarks
- Cuban Missile Crisis
- *Peanuts* cartoon characters
- *Apollo II* astronauts
- Civil Rights Movement
- Great Society
- Counterculture Movement

42

CIVIL RIGHTS MOVEMENT

The 1960s were a time of action in the Civil Rights Movement. Leaders were tired of waiting for legislation to improve their lives, so they planned sit-ins, boycotts, and marches to draw attention to their demands.

Circle the words or dates on the right that match the words on the left.

1. 35th President	Kennedy	Carter	Ford
2. "I Have a Dream . . ." speech	M. L. King, Jr.	Newton	Evers
3. March on Washington	1965	1963	1969
4. Watts Riots	Cincinnati	Boston	Los Angeles
5. Dr. M. L. King, Jr.	nonviolent	Muslim	violent
6. Civil Rights goal	integration	segregation	occupation
7. Sit-in	Washington Capitol rotunda	Woolworth's lunch counter	Atlanta bus station
8. Freedom Rides	car sale	reduced plane fare	bus protest
9. Malcolm X	Black Muslim	Catholic	Baptist
10. Stokely Carmichael	black power	segregation	nonviolence
11. Huey Newton	Freedom Rides	Black Panthers	NAACP
12. Rosa Parks	March on Washington	Montgomery bus boycott	Freedom Rides
13. Medgar Evers	NAACP	Supreme Court justice	famous Civil Rights lawyer
14. "Segregation now, segregation tomorrow, and segregation forever"	George McGovern	Lyndon Johnson	George Wallace
15. Ku Klux Klan	nonviolent political group	supported desegregation	bombed black churches in the South

FLY ME TO THE MOON

The United States joined the space race in the 1960s when President Kennedy promised to put a man on the moon. Write true or false in the blank before the statements. After each false statement, write the word or words that make it true.

1. _____ Russia sent Yuri Gagarin into space in 1969. _____

2. _____ Russia's first spacecraft was called *Mir.* _____

3. _____ Early astronauts wore suits and ties into space. _____

4. _____ There is zero gravity in space. _____

5. _____ The surface of the moon is covered with forests. _____

6. _____ Alan Shepard flew in *Freedom 7.* _____

7. _____ Shepard's flight lasted two days. _____

8. _____ *Gemini 8* practiced docking techniques. _____

9. _____ *Gemini 4* astronauts did not leave their space capsule. _____

10. _____ Cape Canaveral is in Texas. _____

11. _____ Neil Armstrong, Buzz Aldrin, and Michael Collins made the first flight to the
    moon. _____

12. _____ The rocket used in the *Apollo 11* mission was called *Eros.* _____

13. _____ Buzz Aldrin was the first man to walk on the moon. _____

14. _____ It took three weeks to get to the moon. _____

15. _____ Americans watched the moonwalk on their televisions. _____

SCRAMBLED NAMES

The names of these people from the 1960s have been split into two letter segments. The letters of the segments are in order, but the segments are scrambled. Put the pieces together to identify the personality. *Clues are given in parentheses.*

1. FK JO EN HN NE DY (president) _____

2. HU HU BE MP RT EY HR (senator) _____

3. PA AR LM NO ER LD (PGA golfer) _____

4. GA WE PO RY RS (U-2 pilot) _____

5. FL ON OY DP TE AT RS (boxer) _____

6. LY ON ND OH BJ ON NS (senator) _____

7. RI AR CH DN ON IX (presidential candidate) _____

8. RR BA YG DW AT OL ER (senator) _____

9. WI AR LM UD PH OL (female track star) _____

10. KG LE CL AR AB (movie star) _____

11. AL BS AN PA HE RD (astronaut) _____

12. BO YL BD AN (folk singer) _____

13. AN GR AM DM OS ES (artist of rural life) _____

14. LE AR ON DB ER TE NS IN (symphony conductor) _____

15. RT MA IN TH ER LU KI NG (Civil Rights leader) _____

PICTURE PUZZLE

Cut out the individual pieces to make a picture of an important event in American history.

THE TORCH IS PASSED

John F. Kennedy, elected president of the United States in 1961, was shot while riding through the streets of a major city in Texas in 1963. Circle the correct answer to each of the following questions about Kennedy's assassination.

❶ Time of Day	❷ Location	❸ Date
morning	Atlanta	October 15, 1963
afternoon	Cincinnati	November 22, 1963
evening	Dallas	September 7, 1963
midnight	San Diego	May 4, 1963

❹ Weapon	❺ Scene	❻ First Lady
rifle	giving a speech	Ann
handgun	riding in motorcade	Rosemary
knife	eating dinner	Louise
poison	touring Europe	Jacqueline

❼ Vice President	❽ Assassin	❾ Burial Place
Lyndon Johnson	Henry Ford	Forest Lawn
Barry Goldwater	John Wilkes Booth	Arlington
Richard Nixon	Lee Harvey Oswald	Memorial Park
Hubert Humphrey	Fidel Castro	Gate of Heaven

❿ Nationality of Assassin	⓫ Wounded Politician	⓬ Type of Car
Cuban immigrant	John B. Connally	limousine
Soviet defector	Lyndon B. Johnson	sedan
American	Robert F. Kennedy	convertible
German	Dean Rusk	truck

THE PEACE CORPS

Fill in the blanks and fit the answers into the puzzle.

The Peace Corps is a _____ organization.

Volunteers _____ natives how to plant trees.

A participant must be at least 18 years old and a U.S. _____ .

Members agree to serve in the Corps for two _____ .

They must respect the _____ of their host country.

Peace Corps volunteers do not receive a _____ .

It is important that members enjoy _____ and helping people.

Participants must leave their _____ and _____ behind.

The Peace Corps is the "toughest job you'll ever _____ ."

WORDS WITHIN WORDS

Use the clues to help you fill in the blanks with a small word. The answers are words relating to important issues, events, or creations of the seventies. *Clues are given in parentheses.*

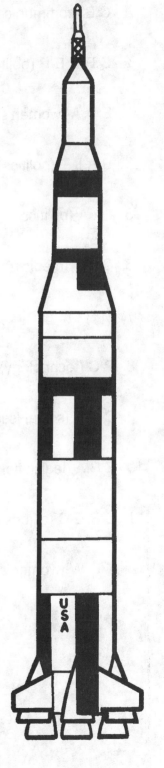

1. __ __ __ T N A M (politics)

2. A __ __ __ __ M E N T (legislation)

3. E N __ __ __ __ __ __ E D (social issue)

4. C O N __ __ __ __ __ __ I O N (legislation)

5. I __ __ __　H O S T __ __ __　C R I S I S (politics)

6. __ __ __ T H　D A Y (social issue)

7. E N V __ __ __ __ M E N T (social issue)

8. F E __ __ __ __ S M (politics)

9. E M __ __ __ G O (politics)

10. C O M __ __ __ E R (technology)

11. S P A C E __ __ __ __ __ (technology)

12. F __ __ __ I O N (social issue)

13. __ __ __ __ __　D __ __ __ __　A C C O R D (politics)

14. W __ __ __ R G __ __ __ (politics)

15. A F __ __ __ __ __ A T I V E　__ __ __ I O N (social issue)

INITIALS AND ACRONYMS

These titles have been shortened to the first letters of each word. Use the clues to help you write the complete titles. *Clues are given in parentheses.*

1. C B (communication) _____

2. C R E E P (politics) _____

3. E R A (women's rights) _____

4. S A L T (politics)_____

5. I R A (politics)_____

6. C A T (medicine) _____

7. M R I (medicine)_____

8. P C (technology)_____

9. C D F (social issue) _____

10. E P A (legislation)_____

11. O P E C (oil crisis) _____

12. N O W (women's rights) _____

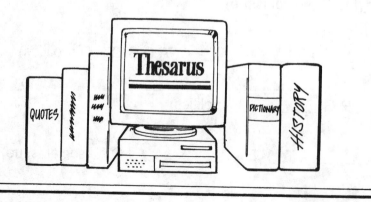

50

HEADLINES

Use a reference book to help you find the person(s) referred to in each of these stories. *There are more people listed in the word bank than you will need.*

1._____ Prime Minister Declares National Emergency—Quebec Separatists Terrorize Workers

2._____ American Swimmer Wins Seven Gold Medals at Munich Games

3._____ VP Resigns After Conspiracy Trial—Nixon Names Ford Successor

4._____ Acclaimed Artist Wraps Fence in San Francisco

5._____ Children's Author Contributes to *Free to Be You and Me* Project for *Ms.* Magazine.

6._____ Miniseries Explains Family History, Realistic Roots

7._____ *Annie Hall* Sweeps Oscars—Director Stars with Diane Keaton

8._____ Russian Dancer Defects—Joins American Ballet Theater

9._____ Feminist Publisher Introduces New Magazine

10._____ First Black Woman Elected to U.S. Senate

11._____ First Lady Opens Clinic for Addicts

12._____ President Pardons Vietnam Draft Dodgers

13._____ President Resigns in Disgrace—Watergate Tapes Prove Conspiracy

14._____ Secretary of State Resigns After Failed Hostage Rescue

15._____ Three American Boxers Win Gold at Montreal Olympics

_____

_____

Word Bank

- Spiro Agnew
- Cyrus Vance
- Richard Nixon
- Pierre Trudeau
- Mark Spitz
- Michael Spinks
- Leon Spinks
- Sugar Ray Leonard
- Jimmy Carter
- Betty Ford
- Shirley Chisholm
- Christo
- Judy Blume
- Alex Haley
- Gloria Steinem
- Woody Allen
- Mikhail Baryshnikov
- Nelson Rockefeller
- Bob Woodward
- George McGovern
- Adam Clayton Powell, Jr.

SPACE EXPLORATION

Write true or false in the blank before the statements. After each false statement, write the word or words that make it true.

1. _____ *Apollo 13* landed safely on the moon. _____

2. _____ *Apollo 13's* lunar module provided backup power and oxygen. _____

3. _____ *Mariner 9* orbited Venus. _____

4. _____ *Apollo 16* and *17* were missions to the moon. _____

5. _____ *Skylab* crews observed the effects of zero gravity on small creatures.

   _____

6. _____ *Skylab* orbited the Earth for three years. _____

7. _____ *Skylab* had eight telescopes. _____

8. _____ *Mariner 10* was a weather satellite. _____

9. _____ *Viking 1* searched for life on Mars. _____

10. _____ *Voyager 1* discovered water on Mars. _____

EARTH DAY

Cross out the words that complete these statements.

1. You can _____ water by taking short showers.
2. Use both sides of paper and then _____ it.
3. Plant a tree. They absorb _____ _____ .
4. Trees give off _____ .
5. _____ products remain in landfills forever.
6. Write to factories about air and water _____ .
7. Support zoos that protect _____ _____ .
8. Save _____ by lowering the thermostat.
9. Try not to buy or use products made from _____ .
10. Turn off _____ when you leave the room.
11. Don't use _____ on your lawn or garden.
12. Repair faucets that _____ .
13. Don't use _____ grocery bags.
14. Don't buy products that have many layers of _____ .
15. Do your part to keep _____ out of landfills.

The celebration of Earth Day was originated to protect the _____ .

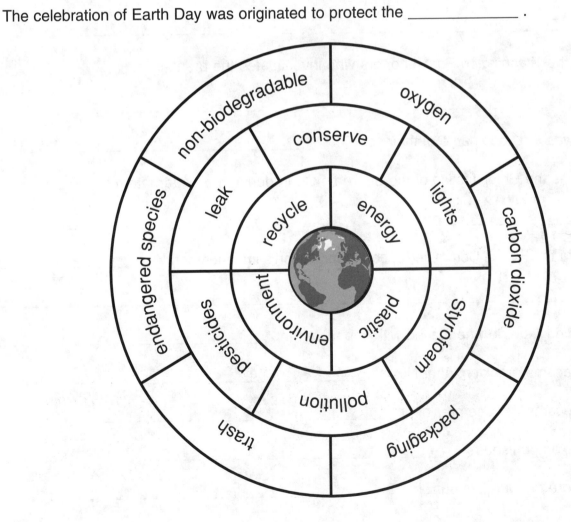

WATERGATE TRIVIA

In 1972 seven men were accused of breaking into the National Democratic Headquarters. This scandal spread to include members of President Richard Nixon's cabinet and finally led to his resignation.

1. Who was the judge at the Watergate trial? _____

2. On what date were the Watergate burglars arrested? _____

3. How many men were indicted in the break-in? _____

4. How many minutes were erased from Nixon's phone tape? _____

5. Who erased the tape? _____

6. Name four members of the Nixon Administration who resigned because of allegations that the White House tried to cover-up the Watergate affair.

   _____   _____

   _____   _____

7. Name the *Washington Post* reporters who investigated the break-in.

   _____   _____

8. What was the code name of their source? _____

9. Who was the Chief Justice of the Supreme Court during the Watergate trial?

   _____

10. Why did the House Committee recommend Nixon's impeachment?_____

    _____

11. What did Nixon do when faced with impeachment? _____

12. Who became president after Nixon? _____

13. Who became the vice president?_____

14. Was Nixon punished? _____

15. How were the burglars punished? _____

54

LISTS

The events, items, and people listed here were newsmakers in the 1980s. Read the lists and fill in the titles.

1. _____
   Greg Louganis
   Matt Biondi
   Janet Evans
   Eric Heiden
   Bonnie Blair

2. _____
   Dr. Sally Ride
   John W. Young
   Robert L. Crippen
   Dr. Judith Resnick
   Michael J. Smith

3. _____
   John Lennon
   Michael Jackson
   Whitney Houston
   Madonna
   Led Zepplin

4. _____
   Mikhail Gorbachev
   Deng Xiaoping
   Ronald Reagan
   Margaret Thatcher
   Anwar el-Sadat

5. _____
   Sandra Day O'Connor
   Geraldine Ferraro
   Nancy Reagan
   Barbara Bush
   Wilma Mankiller

6. _____
   Exxon Valdez
   Chernobyl
   Challenger
   Mount Saint Helens
   Famine in Ethiopia

7. _____
   Soviet troops
   guerillas
   Kabul
   Jimmy Carter
   peace accord

8. _____
   Ronald Reagan
   Mikhail Gorbachev
   START I
   warheads
   missiles

9. _____
   Oliver North
   Ronald Reagan
   Nicaragua
   Sandinistas
   Contras

10. _____
   East/West Germany
   barbed wire
   border
   freedom
   outdoor art galleries

CREATE-A-WORD

Choose a part of a word from each column to form a new word related to the eighties. Each part may be used only once. The first part of of each word is in column A. Write the new words in the blanks.

A	B	C
terr	ri	ist
com	plo	ist
pro	cy	or
hos	dic	es
in	struc	sion
pres	lym	dent
o	i	pics
de	va	tion
ad	tag	sion
ex	test	cling
re	mun	er
bar	or	tion

1. _____

2. _____

3. _____

4. _____

5. _____

6. _____

7. _____

8. _____

9. _____

10. _____

11. _____

12. _____

56

ANALOGIES

To complete an analogy, you must first determine the relationship between the given items. The relationship may be person to birthplace, place to event, inventor to invention, etc. They are read as follows:

Ronald Reagan:Illinois::George Bush:Massachusetts

(Ronald Reagan is to Illinois as George Bush is to Massachusetts)

1. *Indian in the Cupboard*:_____::*Light in the Attic*:Shel Silverstein

2. TWA Flight 847:Rome::Pan Am Flight 103:_____

3. Mikhail Gorbachev:_____::Anwar el-Sadat:Egypt

4. Meryl Streep:_____::Barbara Walters:television

5. Chernobyl:steam explosion::_____:volcanic eruption

6. Eric Heiden:_____::Mary Lou Retton:gymnast

7. *Enterprise*:first orbiter::_____:first shuttle

8. answering machine:_____::VCRs:TV shows

9. John Lennon:Beatles::Michael Jackson:_____

10. Prince Charles:England::Lech Walesa:_____

11. Conservative:Labor::Democratic:_____

12. Jimmy Carter:_____::Ronald Reagan:George Bush

OLYMPIC PEOPLE AND PLACES

Cross out these people and places.

1. She set a world record in winning 500-meter speed skating.
2. He is the first athlete to win 5 individual gold medals at one Olympics.
3. The site of the 1984 winter Olympics
4. The site of the 1984 summer Olympics
5. The site of the 1980 winter Olympics
6. The site of the 1980 summer Olympics
7. The site of the 1988 winter Olympics
8. The site of the 1988 summer Olympics
9. This track and field athlete participated in three Olympics.
10. She won silver and gold medals competing in the heptathlon.
11. This gymnast won the all-round gold medal in the 1984 Olympics.
12. She holds records in three freestyle swimming events.
13. He was the first diver to win springboard and platform events in two Olympics.
14. This wrestler won a gold medal in the freestyle super heavyweight division.
15. This male swimmer won 5 gold, 1 silver, and 1 bronze medal.

The remaining word names the country whose invasion by the Soviet Union caused President Jimmy Carter to ask the Olympic Committee to boycott the games in Moscow.
This country was _____.

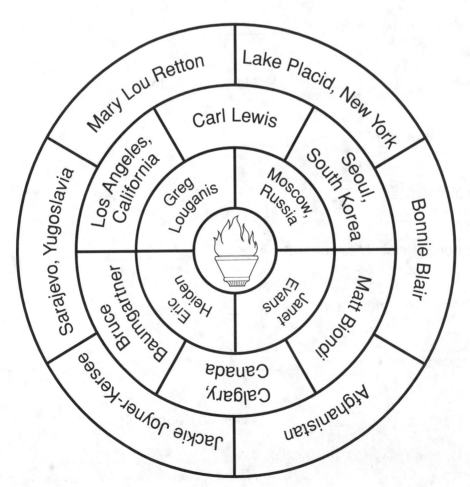

PRESIDENTIAL PUZZLE

Fill in the blanks and fit the answers into the puzzle spaces.

B

N

P

T

F

R O N A L D ▪ **R E A G A N**

W

A

Y

I

He was the 40th _____ of the United States.

He appointed the first _____ to the Supreme Court.

He wanted to cut _____ for all Americans.

John Hinckley attempted to _____ him.

His wife is named _____ .

He sent aid to freedom fighters in _____ .

He thought it was important to balance the federal _____ .

He was a movie _____ .

He signed a treaty with the _____ to reduce nuclear arsenals.

He proposed a missile shield called _____ _____.

CHALLENGER SHUTTLE DISASTER

The *Challenger* shuttle flew nine successful missions. On its tenth flight on January 28, 1986, *Challenger* exploded less than two minutes after take-off, killing all the crew members. Write true or false in the blank before the statements. After each false statement, write the word or words that make it true.

_____ 1. Space shuttles have three parts: an orbiter, external tank, and solid fuel rocket boosters._____

_____ 2. The *Challenger* exploded on January 28, 1986._____

_____ 3. The *Challenger* had successfully completed six flights before the explosion.

_____

_____ 4. Eight astronauts were lost aboard the space shuttle *Challenger*._____

_____

_____ 5. Christa McAuliffe was a high school social studies teacher on board the ill-fated flight._____

_____ 6. George Bush was president at the time of the accident. _____

_____ 7. The explosion was caused by a gas leak from a faulty seal in the solid fuel rocket booster._____

_____ 8. Cold weather at launch time contributed to the accident._____

_____

_____ 9. The disaster happened 74 seconds after liftoff. _____

_____

_____ 10. A report said NASA had no idea about problems with the design of the shuttle._____

_____ 11. The bodies of the astronauts were recovered and buried at Arlington National Cemetery. _____

_____ 12. The *Discovery* shuttle was launched successfully 2 ½ years following the *Challenger* disaster. _____

60

INITIALS AND ACRONYMS

These titles have been shortened to the first letters of each word. Use the clues to help you write the complete titles. *Clues are given in parentheses.*

1. U S S R _____ (world—Asia)

2. P L O _____ (world—Mideast)

3. U N _____ (world)

4. A N C _____ (civil rights—Africa)

5. C D-R O M _____ (technology)

6. D I N K S _____ (social)

7. W W W _____ (technology)

8. N A T O _____ (world politics)

9. M S - D O S _____ (technology)

10. N A S A _____ (science)

11. I B M _____ (technology)

12. P G A _____ (sports)

13. N A A C P _____ (civil rights)

14. R O T C _____ (army)

15. E D S _____ (technology)

ANALOGIES

To complete an analogy, you must first determine the relationship between the given items. The relationship may be person to birthplace, place to event, inventor to invention, etc. They are read as follows:

Michael Jordan:basketball::Tiger Woods:golf

(Michael Jordan is to basketball as Tiger Woods is to golf)

1. Janet Reno:Harvard Law School::Hillary Clinton:_____

2. Ross Perot:_____::Bill Clinton:Democrat

3. Louis Farrakhan:Nation of Islam::Rev. Benjamin Chavis:_____

4. _____:Magic Johnson::hockey:Wayne Gretzky

5. Bill Gates:_____::Ted Turner:CNN

6. Johnny Carson:Iowa::Oprah Winfrey:_____

7. Janet Reno:attorney general::Madeline Albright:_____

8. Boris Yeltsin:Russia::_____:United States

9. Michael Johnson:running::Dan Jansen:_____

10. Pete Sampras:_____::Oprah Winfrey:microphone

11. George Bush:_____::Bill Clinton:Al Gore

12. Yitzhak Rabin:_____::Nelson Mandela:South Africa

13. *Titanic*:_____::*Schindler's List*:Steven Spielberg

14. Tony Blair:_____::Benjamin Netanyahu:Israel

WEB SITES

These imaginary Web sites could lead you to information about famous people of the 1990s. Answer each one with a name.

1. www.russia.pres.gov_____

2. www.firstlady.US_____

3. www.mmmarch.wash/LF_____

4. www.masters1997/PGA_____

5. www.chmn/USJCS./Bush_____

6. www.1stfem/attorneygen.US_____

7. www.reformpty.pres._____

8. www.bullsstar/MJ.nike_____

9. www.windows/MS_____

10. www.woman/NASA.*Mir*_____

11. www.daytime/talk/abc_____

12. www.primeminister.Isr/Nobel_____

13. www.pres.safrica_____

14. www.ussr/fmr.pres_____

15 www.leader/PLO_____

LISTS

The events, items, and people listed here were all important in the 1990s. Read the lists and fill in the titles.

1. _____
   U.S. terrorism
   Murrah Federal Building
   truck bomb
   Timothy McVeigh
   Terry Nichols

2. _____
   Kuwait
   Saudi Arabia
   Norman Schwarzkopf
   Iraq
   Saddam Hussein

3. _____
   Louis Farrakhan
   black men
   responsibility
   Rev. Benjamin Chavis
   Washington, D.C.

4. _____
   Shannon Lucid, NASA
   Mir Space Station
   Russian cooperation
   scientific experiments
   cosmonauts

5. _____
   rhyming verse
   strong beat
   no melody
   MTV
   sampling

6. _____
   Muslims
   Serbs
   Croats
   bombs
   peace negotiations

7. _____
   coup
   Yeltsin
   Gorbachev
   Kremlin
   perestroika (economic reform)

8. _____
   Gaza Strip
   West Bank
   PLO, Yasir Arafat
   Yitzhak Rabin
   Shimon Peres

9. _____
   Nelson Mandela
   segregation
   African National Congress
   white minority rule
   independence

10. _____
   U.S. Dept. of Defense
   e-mail
   on-line
   download
   modem

64

GULF WAR

Analyze the code to find the answers.

Code	25	26	1	2	3	4	5	6	7	8	9	10	11	12	13	14	15	16	17	18	19	20	21	22	23	24
Key	A	B	C	D	E	F	G	H	I	J	K	L	M	N	O	P	Q	R	S	T	U	V	W	X	Y	Z

Example: 7-16-25-15 <u>Iraq</u>

1. **code name**

   13-14-3-16-25-18-7-13-12   2-3-17-3-16-18   17-18-13-16-11

   _____   _____   _____

2. **people**

   17-25-2-2-25-11   6-19-17-17-3-7-12

   _____   _____

   12-13-16-11-25-12   17-1-6-21-25-16-24-9-13-14-4

   _____   _____

   14-16-3-17-7-2-3-12-18   5-3-13-16-5-3   26-19-17-6

   _____   _____   _____

3. **places**

   26-25-5-6-2-25-2 _____

   9-19-21-25-7-18 _____

   21-25-17-6-7-12-5-18-13-12   2-1

   _____   _____

4. **weapons**

   17-1-19-2   11-7-17-17-7-10-3

   _____   _____

   17-18-3-25-10-18-6   4-7-5-6-18-3-16

   _____   _____

   18-13-11-25-6-25-21-9   1-16-19-7-17-3   11-7-17-17-7-10-3

   _____   _____   _____

   1-13-11-26-25-18   25-7-16-1-16-25-4-18

   _____   _____

CURRENT EVENTS

Analyze these clues to determine the events.

1. France and England worked together on this project.
   It is more than 30 miles from end to end.
   Machines with steel teeth were used to cut through soft rock.
   It connects Folkestone, England, and Calais, France.
   This underwater transportation was opened May 6, 1994.

   What is the event? _____

2. The Berlin Wall has fallen; the Soviet influence is gone.
   People cheered and families are reunited.
   Chancellor Helmut Kohl is the head of the new government.
   Berlin will be the new capital.
   East and West are one nation again.

   What is the event? _____

3. Iraqi tanks across the border.
   U.N. leaders condemn the invasion.
   The U.S. sends war ships.
   The palace is burned; the emir escapes to Saudi Arabia.
   What is the event? _____

4. Human barricades save the Russian Parliament.
   Three Muscovites are killed by tanks.
   The Communist Party is shut down.
   Party leaders resign.
   Boris Yeltsin is a hero.
   What is the event? _____

5. His democratic reform movement began the new system.
   Eleven former Soviet republics became the Commonwealth of Independent States.
   Control of the Soviet nuclear arsenal passed to Yeltsin.
   The red flag was lowered over the Kremlin; his job was abolished.
   What is the event? _____

6. Terrorist attack New York City.
   The Twin Towers garage is believed to be the site of the bomb.
   Five are killed; many suffer smoke inhalation.
   Fire rages in commuter train station.
   What is the event? _____

66

R.I.P.

Here are sayings, or epitaphs, that might have appeared on the tombstones of famous people throughout the twentieth century. Read the clues and fill in their names. Use a reference book to determine the year each one died.

1. With Bible and hatchet she fought the sale of liquor and tobacco.

   Here lies _____ 1846 – _____

2. Her pictures and stories about small woodland animals bring enjoyment to young children.

   Here lies _____ 1866 – _____

3. As a professional baseball player, this "Georgia Peach" won 12 batting titles.

   Here lies _____ 1886 – _____

4. America's sweetheart appeared in 194 films and won an Academy Award in 1928.

   Here lies _____ 1893 – _____

5. This military scout and sharpshooter starred in his own Wild West show.

   Here lies _____ 1846 – _____

6. This "Little Tramp" made American audiences laugh in silent movies.

   Here lies _____ 1889 – _____

7. She was lost while flying solo across the Atlantic Ocean.

   Here lies _____ 1897 – _____

8. He was the first African American to integrate major league baseball and play in a World Series.

   Here lies _____ 1919 – _____

9. This "Argentine Joan of Arc" married the president even though she had not finished high school.

   Here lies _____ 1919 – _____

10. Half of a husband-wife comedy team, her career began on the vaudeville stage.

    Here lies _____ 1906 – _____

Word Bank

- Gracie Allen-1964
- Evita Peron-1952
- Jackie Robinson-1972
- Charlie Chaplin-1977
- Buffalo Bill Cody-1917
- Mary Pickford-1979
- Amelia Earhart-1937
- Beatrix Potter-1943
- Carry Nation-1911
- Ty Cobb-1961

NICKNAMES

Match the real names of the people in the word bank with their nicknames. *Clues are given in parentheses.*

1. Sultan of Swat _____ (baseball)

2. The Black Pearl _____ (soccer)

3. Ike _____ (president)

4. Dutch _____ (president)

5. The Cos _____ (entertainer)

6. The Iron Lady _____ (prime minister)

7. The King of Late Night _____ (entertainer)

8. The Golden Bear _____ (golf)

9. The Wizard of Menlo Park _____ (inventor)

10. Bubba _____ (president)

11. Satchmo _____ (musician)

12. Georgia Peach _____ (baseball)

13. Little Tramp _____ (entertainer)

14. America's Sweetheart _____ (entertainer)

15. Scarface _____ (gangster)

Word Bank

• Babe Ruth	• Mary Pickford	• Margaret Thatcher
• Pelé	• Charlie Chaplain	• Johnny Carson
• Dwight Eisenhower	• Ty Cobb	• Jack Nicklaus
• Ronald Reagan	• Louis Armstrong	• Thomas Edison
• Bill Cosby	• Bill Clinton	• Al Capone

68

FAMOUS PAIRS

Find out who these famous pairs are by using the clues given below.

1. These archaeologists uncovered fossils of early man at Olduvai Gorge, Tanzania.

   They are _____

2. These German immigrants collaborated on the *Curious George* books.

   They are _____

3. These Argentine leaders are remembered as saints in their native country.

   They are _____

4. Charged with treason for passing secrets to the Soviet Union during World War II, this couple was sentenced to death.

   They are _____

5. These comedians had a show business career in vaudeville, radio, and television.

   They are _____

6. This first couple lived in the White House longer than any other.

   They are _____

7. These brothers wrote the music and lyrics for many popular songs of the 1920s.

   They are _____

8. These explorers were the first to reach the North Pole.

   They are _____

9. This former president and first lady once had careers as movie actors.

   They are _____

10. This royal couple's divorce caused concern about the future of Britain's monarchy.

    They are _____

11. These woman of Northern Ireland won the Nobel Peace Prize for their work against violence.

    They are _____

12. These men worked in Panama to make it possible for America to build the Panama Canal.

    They are _____

WEB SITES

These imaginary Web sites could lead you to information about famous people, places, or events in the twentieth century. Find the person, place, or thing that would be closely linked to the following imaginary Web sites.

1. www.daviscup.com _____

2. www.worldcup.1958 _____

3. www.volcanoes.us.washington _____

4. www.oilspill.alaska.exx/val _____

5. www.reunification.ger/wall _____

6. www.tuskegee.sch.edu _____

7. www.saturday-evening-post.covers.art _____

8. www.cherokee.nation.fem.chief _____

9. www.landmarks.syd.au _____

10. www.nasa.moonwalk.gov _____

11. www.vatican-city/head _____

12. www.1stfem/SCourt.US _____

13. www.greatsociety/US.pres _____

14. www.scandal/resign.Nixon _____

15. www.lennon-mccartney/music.group _____

QUOTES AND SLOGANS

Match the president to his quote or campaign slogan. *There are more presidents listed than there are campaign slogans.*

1._____ *I like Ike.*

2._____ *Four more lucky years*

3._____ *LBJ for the USA*

4._____ *Speak softly and carry a big stick.*

5._____ *Four more years of a full dinner pail*

6._____ *I'm voting for Betty's husband.*

7._____ *The buck stops here.*

8._____ *The morning in America.*

9._____ *Read my lips: No new taxes!*

10._____ *We must build a bridge to the future.*

- Gerald Ford
- Woodrow Wilson
- Richard Nixon
- Franklin D. Roosevelt
- Bill Clinton
- Teddy Roosevelt
- George Bush

- Harry Truman
- William McKinley
- Ronald Reagan
- Lyndon B. Johnson
- Dwight Eisenhower
- Herbert Hoover
- Calvin Coolidge

EQUATIONS

In an equation one side always equals the other. Fill in these equations to find out what in twentieth century history is equal to each other. *Clues are given in parentheses.*

1. 9 = P on a BT (*1900 World Series*)= _____ Players on a baseball team _____

2. 9 = S integrating LRCHS (*civil rights*) = _____

3. 4 = P on MR (*national memorial in South Dakota*) = _____

4. 4 = S killed at KSU (*1970 Vietnam War protest*) = _____

5. 110,000 = JA confined during WWII (*1940s war*) = _____

6. 50 = S in the U.S. (*North America*) = _____

7. 18 = LA to V (*politics*) = _____

8. 58,000 = A died in VW (*1960s–70s war*) = _____

9. 4 = B recorded R&R music (*1960s entertainment*) = _____

10. 159 = C in the UN (*world politics*) = _____

11. 3 = times JG orbitted E (*space technology*) = _____

12. 43 = JFK's age when elected P (*1960s politics*) = _____

13. 4 = times FDR elected P (*1940s politics*) = _____

14. 28 = years G divided by BW (*cold war*) = _____

15. 3 = AP in WWII (*1940s war*) = _____

72

FASHION SHOW

Write the decade for each style of clothing.

1._____

3._____

2._____

FASHION SHOW *(cont.)*

Write the decade for each style of clothing.

4._____

6._____

5._____

ANSWER KEY

Page 3
1. Elizabeth Stanton
2. Teddy Roosevelt
3. Mohandas Gandhi
4. Albert Einstein
5. Sigmund Freud
6. Rudyard Kipling
7. Pablo Picasso
8. Will Rogers
9. Anna Jarvis
10. Andrew Carnegie
11. Wilbur Wright
12. Lucy Maud Montgomery

Page 4
Answers will vary.

Page 5
1. automobile
2. temperance
3. New York
4. soccer
5. tank
6. Russia
7. Einstein
8. *The Tale of Peter Rabbit*
9. cubism
10. radio
11. Father's Day
12. Native Americans
13. United States
14. China
15. theater production

Page 6
1. prisoners
2. Aborigines
3. Canberra
4. states
5. continent
6. Britain
7. gold
8. Sydney

Page 7
1. Henri de Toulouse-Lautrec 1901
2. Paul Gaugin 1903
3. James Whistler 1903
4. Frederick Bartholdi 1904
5. Jules Verne 1905
6. Henrik Ibsen 1906
7. Paul Cézanne 1906
8. Nicolai Rimsky-Korsakov 1908
9. Joel Chandler Harris 1908

10. Antonin Dvorak 1904

Page 8
1. Lyman Frank Baum
2. Andrew Carnegie
3. Oklahoma Territory
4. William McKinley
5. Panama
6. Theodore Roosevelt
7. New York City
8. Henry Ford
9. Boston
10. William Howard Taft
11. Robert Peary
12. Geronimo
13. London
14. Rudyard Kipling
15. Ellis Island

Page 9
1. Wilson
2. Taft
3. Wilson
4. Taft
5. Taft
6. Taft
7. Taft
8. Wilson
9. Wilson
10. Taft
11. Wilson
12. Wilson
13. Wilson
14. Taft
15. Taft
16. Wilson
17. Wilson
18. Taft
19. Wilson
20. Taft

Page 10
1. Allies
2. tanks
3. enemy
4. submarine
5. army
6. force
7. march
8. target
9. invade
10. attack
11. Germany
12. Balkans

Page 11
1. limiting child labor
2. shortened work day
3. safe working conditions
4. increased wages
5. creation of labor unions
6. worker strikes
7. industrial revolution
8. mass production
9. job security
10. pension funds

Page 12
1. kinetophone
2. Panama Canal
3. *Lusitania*
4. Vladimir Lenin
5. *Titanic*

6. Olympics
7. Father's Day
8. epidemic (pandemic)
9. alcohol
10. right to vote
11. League of Nations
12. child labor

Page 13
1. Vincenzo Perugia
2. Roald Amundsen
3. Madame Marie Curie
4. Dr. William Gorgas
5. Gavrilo Princip
6. Jack Johnson
7. German submarine
8. Bolshevik forces
9. French officials
10. Max Planck
11. Benito Mussolini
12. Germany and Allied leaders
13. Woodrow Wilson
14. Constantine I
15. Turks of the Ottoman Empire

Page 14
1. *Titanic*
2. *Carpathia*
3. *California*
4. New York City
5. iceberg
6. Captain Edward Smith
7. Belfast, Ireland
8. John Jacob Astor

Page 15

Page 16
1. I, sound
2. C, silent
3. F, sound
4. A, silent
5. H, silent
6. J, silent
7. K, silent
8. G, silent
9. L, sound
10. E, silent
11. D, silent
12. B, sound

ANSWER KEY (cont.)

Page 17
immigration, suffragism, temperance, alcohol, bootlegging, demonstrate, prejudice, creationism, religion, amendment, bigotry, liberty

Page 18
1. Al Capone
2. Prohibition
3. flappers
4. Jazz
5. Ku Klux Klan
6. Oct.29, 1929
7. speakeasies
8. Jack Dempsey, Lou Gehrig
9. Model T
10. Gloria Swanson, Greta Garbo
11. Amelia Earhart, Gertrude Stein
12. zipper, pop-up toaster
13. Harding, Coolidge
14. Margaret Sanger, Ethel Byrne
15. Clarence Darrow, William Jennings Bryan

Roaring Twenties

Page 19
1. zipper
2. Wrigley's chewing gum
3. Band-Aids
4. Kleenex
5. Scotch tape
6. potato chips
7. frozen vegetables
8. permanent wave
9. Eskimo Pie
10. Welch's grape jelly

Page 20
1. Babe Ruth
2. "Shoeless" Joe Jackson
3. Warren G. Harding
4. Sacco and Vanzetti
5. Tutankhamen
6. Vladimir Lenin
7. John Scopes
8. Harry Houdini
9. Charles Lindbergh
10. Duke Ellington
11. Amelia Earhart
12. Emperor Hirohito
13. Coco Chanel
14. Commander Richard Byrd
15. Alexander Fleming

Page 21
1. Valley of the Kings
2. Luxor, Egypt
3. Howard Carter
4. Lord Carnarvon
5. embroidered robes
6. gilt statues
7. precious stones
8. Pharaoh's tomb
9. four chariots
10. hieroglyphic writing
11. golden mummy case

Page 22
1. Harvard
2. highways
3. gangster
4. investors
5. Margaret Mitchell
6. track and field
7. clarinet
8. song
9. quintuplets
10. Germany
11. actress
12. Alexander Calder
13. Metropolitan Opera
14. Franklin Roosevelt
15. Wallis Simpson

Page 23
1. Herbert and Lou Hoover
2. Franklin and Eleanor Roosevelt
3. Lou Henry Hoover
4. George Washington Carver
5. Jane Addams
6. Shirley Temple
7. Woody Guthrie
8. Babe Didrikson
9. Sergei Prokofiev
10. John Steinbeck
11. Edward VIII
12. Superman

Page 24
1. "A chicken in every pot: A car in every garage."
2. "We have nothing to fear but fear itself."
3. "Our greatest primary task is to put people to work."

Page 25
Berlin Olympics
Los Angeles medals

Page 26
1. Great Depression
2. labor unions
3. prohibition
4. migration
5. helicopter
6. Hoovervilles
7. unemployment
8. president
9. Social Security
10. Adolf Hitler

Page 27
1. Monopoly
2. yo-yo
3. roller skates
4. jump rope
5. frozen food
6. Spam
7. Wonder bread
8. Snow White and the Seven Dwarfs
9. television
10. Superman

Page 28
1. Pearl Harbor
2. rationing coupons
3. Rosie the Riveter
4. Winston Churchill
5. Franklin Roosevelt
6. Axis Powers
7. Douglas MacArthur
8. Poland

Page 29
Answers will vary.

Page 30
1. Allied Forces
2. Axis Powers
3. atomic bomb
4. home front
5. rationed items
6. heroes
7. world leaders
8. aircrafts
9. battles
10. Holocaust

Page 31

1. 12/7/41	6. 5/10/40
2. 1/20/45	7. 6/6/44
3. 10/29/40	8. 1/27/45
4. 2/19/45	9. 4/30/45
5. 4/12/45	10. 8/14/45

Page 32

big band music
theater

Page 33

```
J N P E Q K T R M Y W I C P Q & M F A J N I Q
P S T L I U S X O S T L A N G W K P E R O S T
E A L B E C T V D E B R U K J M I B U W X O K
N I G U A O U R I C & J G H E T O G N A C L A
P K C I L L G F X I D A F A O Y U K R H I D R
W X A T S I D H E O U C N I & L X A S W E J A
H M L E H N A F & M M O V W Z V C P J Z E P B
I N & T Y G I V T U P C U N I M U T T G F D C
P S M J N A P I E R K A B S L Y P A Y K I A M
Q X W I L U E M K U L T X O L L U B I L U R O
R Q E S G Q R & J L O P R U Z M Q R O N O T E
E L M R J Z K M Q A S W I V S A N S & S P J Z
I B E B U O Y C G R T R A & T R C I H I A R P
W X Q U L X K T S W O I D X B P D S T N C L S
L Z Y S L I N U N X M A C W A K M F O P E F T
& F E P J B K F A R E G H Z Y L R D R E K J Z
```

Page 34

1. baby boomers, beat generation
2. Hawaii, Alaska
3. polio vaccine, kidney transplant
4. color television, major league baseball
5. Billy Graham, Pope John Paul XXIII

Page 35

1. Frisbee
2. *Mad Magazine*
3. Barbie doll
4. rock 'n' roll
5. TV dinner
6. Hula-Hoop
7. Scrabble
8. *Charlotte's Web*
9. Dr. Seuss
10. Jif peanut butter

Page 36

1. H	8. A	15. A
2. H	9. H	16. H
3. A	10. H or A	17. A
4. A	11. A	18. A
5. A	12. H	19. A
6. H	13. A	20. H
7. H	14. H	

Page 37

1. Chuck Berry
2. "Rock Around the Clock"
3. "Teen Angel"
4. "Sixteen Tons"
5. "Unchained Melody"
6. Fats Domino
7. "Jailhouse Rock"
8. "Tears on My Pillow"
9. "Heartbreak Hotel"
10. "Sixteen Candles"

Page 38

1. source and inspiration for King's nonviolent resistance
2. married King in 1953
3. arrested in 1955 in Montgomery which was catalyst for bus boycott
4. Southern Christian Leadership Conference; organized in 1957 to expand nonviolent struggle against racism; King was the first president
5. site of protests led by King against segregation and discrimination
6. confessed to assassination of King on April 4, 1968
7. disciple and follower of King; went into politics
8. successor to King as president of SCLC
9. site of protests against restraints on voter registration
10. site where King received the Nobel Peace Prize

Page 39

1. Billy Graham
2. *Twenty-One*
3. Bess Truman
4. Gen. Douglas MacArthur
5. Hawaii
6. Ethel and Julius Rosenberg
7. Rosa Parks
8. 22nd Amendment
9. Korean War
10. Little Rock Nine
11. Althea Gibson
12. Joe DiMaggio
13. *Explorer I*
14. Mary Leakey
15. Buddy Holly, Ritchie Valens, J.P. Richardson

Page 40

1. Lady Bird
2. prime minister
3. athlete (runner)
4. Washington, D.C.
5. astronaut
6. children's books
7. Israel
8. Charles Schultz
9. Russia
10. Hollywood
11. *Black Judgement,* Rachel Carson
12. surgeon, patient, Denise Duvall
13. Soviet Union
14. Yuri Gagarin

Page 41

1. "Moon River"
2. "Yellow Submarine"
3. Ringo Starr
4. Jefferson Airplane
5. "Cathy's Clown"
6. Rolling Stones
7. Woodstock
8. Three Dog Night
9. "California Dreamin' "
10. "I Left My Heart in San Francisco"

Page 42

1. Vietnam War
2. Civil Rights Movement
3. assassinated leaders
4. *Apollo 11* astronauts
5. parts of a microwave oven
6. *Peanuts* cartoon characters
7. Beatles albums
8. Cuban Missile Crisis
9. celebrities born in the 1960s
10. moon landmarks
11. African American actors
12. subjects of Andy Warhol's paintings
13. Great Society
14. Counterculture Movement
15. popular literary works

ANSWER KEY (cont.)

Page 43
1. Kennedy
2. Martin Luther King, Jr.
3. 1963
4. Los Angeles
5. nonviolent
6. integration
7. Woolworth's lunch counter
8. bus protest
9. Black Muslim
10. black power
11. Black Panthers
12. Montgomery bus boycott
13. NAACP
14. George Wallace
15. bombed black churches in the South

Page 44
1. F, 1961
2. F, *Sputnik*
3. F, spacesuits
4. T
5. F, rocks
6. T
7. F, 15 minutes
8. T
9. F, Edward White walked outside.
10. F, Florida
11. T
12. F, *Saturn*
13. F, Neil Armstrong
14. F, three days
15. T

Page 45
1. John F. Kennedy
2. Hubert Humphrey
3. Arnold Palmer
4. Gary Powers
5. Floyd Patterson
6. Lyndon B. Johnson
7. Richard Nixon
8. Barry Goldwater
9. Wilma Rudolph
10. Clark Gable
11. Alan B. Shepard
12. Bob Dylan
13. Grandma Moses
14. Leonard Bernstein
15. Martin Luther King

Page 46

Page 47
1. afternoon
2. Dallas
3. November 22, 1963
4. rifle
5. riding in a motorcade
6. Jacqueline
7. Lyndon Johnson
8. Lee Harvey Oswald
9. Arlington
10. American
11. John B. Connally
12. convertible

Page 48

Page 49
1. Vietnam
2. amendment
3. endangered
4. conscription
5. Iran hostage crisis
6. Earth Day
7. environment
8. feminism
9. embargo
10. computer
11. spacecraft
12. fashion
13. Camp David Accord
14. Watergate

15. Affirmative Action

Page 50
1. citizens band radio
2. Committee to Reelect the President
3. Equal Rights Amendment
4. Strategic Arms Limitation Talks
5. Irish Republican Army
6. computerized axial tomography
7. magnetic resonance imaging
8. personal computer
9. Children's Defense Fund
10. Environmental Protection Agency
11. Organization of Petroleum Exporting Countries
12. National Organization of Women

Page 51
1. Pierre Trudeau
2. Mark Spitz
3. Spiro Agnew
4. Christo
5. Judy Blume
6. Alex Haley
7. Woody Allen
8. Mikhail Baryshnikov
9. Gloria Steinem
10. Shirley Chisholm
11. Betty Ford
12. Jimmy Carter
13. Richard Nixon
14. Cyrus Vance
15. Michael Spinks, Leon Spinks, Sugar Ray Leonard

Page 52
1. F, the command module lost oxygen and the flight returned to Earth
2. T
3. F, Mars
4. T
5. T
6. F, five years
7. T
8. F, it transmitted pictures of Venus and Mercury
9. T
10. F, it discovered rings around Jupiter

ANSWER KEY (cont.)

Page 53
1. conserve
2. recycle
3. carbon dioxide
4. oxygen
5. non-biodegradable
6. pollution
7. endangered species
8. energy
9. Styrofoam
10. lights
11. pesticides
12. leak
13. plastic
14. packaging
15. trash
environment

Page 54
1. John Sirica
2. June 17, 1972
3. seven
4. 18 minutes
5. Rose Mary Woods
6. H.R. Haldeman, John Erlichman, Richard Kleindinst, John Dean
7. Carl Bernstein, Bob Woodward
8. Deep Throat
9. Chief Justice Warren Burger
10. obstructing justice
11. He resigned.
12. Gerald Ford
13. Nelson Rockefeller
14. No, Ford pardoned Nixon.
15. They served time in prison.

Page 55
1. Olympic Gold Medalists
2. Astronauts
3. Singers/Musicians
4. World Leaders
5. Famous Women
6. Disasters
7. Afghanistan
8. Star Wars
9. Iran-Contra
10. Berlin Wall

Page 56
addiction, terrorist, communist, protestor, explosion, hostages, invasion, president, olympics, recycling, barrier, destruction

Page 57
1. Lynne Reid Banks
2. New York City
3. Russia
4. movies
5. Mount Saint Helens
6. speed skater
7. *Columbia*
8. phone messages
9. Jackson Five
10. Poland
11. Republican
12. Walter Mondale

Page 58
1. Bonnie Blair
2. Eric Heiden
3. Sarajevo, Yugoslavia
4. Los Angeles, California
5. Lake Placid, New York
6. Moscow, Soviet Union
7. Calgary, Canada
8. Seoul, South Korea
9. Carl Lewis
10. Jackie Joyner-Kersee
11. Mary Lou Retton
12. Janet Evans
13. Greg Louganis
14. Bruce Baumgartner
15. Matt Biondi
Afghanistan

Page 59

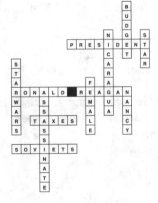

Page 60
1. T
2. T
3. F, there had been 9 flights
4. F, there were seven astronauts
5. T
6. F, Ronald Reagan was

president
7. T
8. F, weather had no effect
9. T
10. F, NASA knew the seals were a problem
11. F, the bodies were never found
12. T

Page 61
1. Union of Soviet Socialist Republics
2. Palestine Liberation Organization
3. United Nations
4. African National Congress
5. compact disk read-only memory
6. double income no kids
7. World Wide Web
8. North Atlantic Treaty Organization
9. Microsoft Disk Operating System
10. National Aeronautic and Space Administration
11. International Business Machines
12. Professional Golfers' Association
13. National Association for the Advancement of Colored People
14. Reserve Officers Training Corps
15. Electronic Data Systems

Page 62
1. Yale Law School
2. Independent
3. NAACP
4. basketball
5. Microsoft
6. Mississippi
7. Secretary of State
8. Bill Clinton
9. speed skating
10. tennis racket
11. Dan Quayle
12. Israel
13. James Cameron
14. England

ANSWER KEY (cont.)

Page 63
1. Boris Yeltsen
2. Hillary Clinton
3. Louis Farrakhan
4. Tiger Woods
5. General Colin Powell
6. Janet Reno
7. Ross Perot
8. Michael Jordan
9. Bill Gates
10. Shannon Lucid
11. Oprah Winfrey
12. Yitzhak Rabin
13. Nelson Mandela
14. Mikhail Gorbachev
15. Yasir Arafat

Page 64
1. Oklahoma City Bombing
2. Persian Gulf War/Operation Desert Storm
3. Million Man March
4. joint U.S.–Russian space program
5. Hip Hop/Rap Music
6. Bosnian War
7. Fall of USSR
8. Palestinian-Israeli Peace Accord
9. End of Apartheid
10. Internet

Page 65
1. Operation Desert Storm
2. Saddam Hussein, Norman Schwarzkopf, President George Bush
3. Baghdad, Kuwait, Washington, D.C.
4. scud missile, stealth fighter, Tomahawk cruise missile, combat aircraft

Page 66
1. building of the Eurotunnel
2. German reunification
3. beginning of the Gulf War
4. Kremlin coup attempt
5. Gorbachev's resignation
6. World Trade Center bombing

Page 67
1. Carry Nation-1911
2. Beatrix Potter-1943
3. Ty Cobb-1961
4. Mary Pickford-1979
5. Buffalo Bill Cody-1917
6. Charlie Chaplin-1977
7. Amelia Earhart-1937
8. Jackie Robinson-1972
9. Evita Peron-1952
10. Gracie Allen-1964

Page 68
1. Babe Ruth
2. Pelé
3. Dwight Eisenhower
4. Ronald Reagan
5. Bill Cosby
6. Margaret Thatcher
7. Johnny Carson
8. Jack Nicklaus
9. Thomas Edison
10. Bill Clinton
11. Louis Armstrong
12. Ty Cobb
13. Charlie Chaplin
14. Mary Pickford
15. Al Capone

Page 69
1. Mary and Louis Leakey
2. Hans and Margaret Rey
3. Juan and Evita Peron
4. Julius and Ethel Rosenberg
5. George Burns and Gracie Allen
6. Franklin and Eleanor Roosevelt
7. George and Ira Gershwin
8. Robert Peary and Matthew Henson
9. Ronald and Nancy Reagan
10. Charles and Diana
11. Mairead Corrigan and Betty Williams
12. General George Goethals and General William Gorgas

Page 70
1. tennis
2. soccer
3. Mount Saint Helens
4. *Exxon-Valdez*
5. Berlin Wall
6. George Washington Carver, Booker T. Washington
7. Norman Rockwell
8. Wilma Mankiller
9. Sydney Opera House
10. Neil Armstrong
11. Pope John Paul II
12. Sandra Day O'Conner
13. Lyndon B. Johnson
14. Watergate
15. The Beatles

Page 71
1. Eisenhower
2. F. D. Roosevelt
3. Johnson
4. Teddy Roosevelt
5. McKinley
6. Ford
7. Truman
8. Reagan
9. Bush
10. Clinton

Page 72
1. players on a baseball team
2. students integrating Little Rock Central High School
3. presidents on Mount Rushmore
4. students killed at Kent State University
5. Japanese Americans confined during World War II
6. states in the United States
7. legal age to vote
8. Americans died in the Vietnam War
9. Beatles recorded rock and roll music
10. countries in the United Nations
11. times John Glenn orbited Earth
12. John Fitzgerald Kennedy's age when elected president
13. times Franklin Delano Roosevelt elected president
14. years Germany was divided by the Berlin Wall
15. Allied Powers in World War II

Pages 73–74
1. 1920
2. 1950
3. 1940
4. 1900
5. 1970
6. 1960 and/or 1970